I0491764

Book Description

Dance to the Tune of Morals approaches the subject of manager-employee relationship with objectivity and the same empathy that it requires. Great dancers move with the flow of the music and tune into the rhythm that surrounds them all while incorporating bass, balance, and tempo. A manager works in a similar way to take in the attributes of the workplace and "tune" it towards success. Not everyone is a great dancer, and not just anyone can be a good manager. This book seeks to enlighten you on the connection between workplace culture and keeping productivity up as a leader. It also explains which qualities the "right" culture must have and how to establish it. Among the chapters in this book you will find topics covering:

- Why kindness is key.
- Different types of management styles.
- The golden rules for business etiquette.
- What defines emotional intelligence.

Managers will find a renewed appreciation for their employees and the knowledge on how to beautifully navigate the dance floor of business with their team.

Dance to the Tune of   Morals

A Manager's Guide to Well-Being & Success

Kirina Nikola Archer MBA, MHA

Table of Contents

Introduction

A company's choice of manager is one of the most crucial decisions it will make. The past successes of a business and stellar qualifications of its workers will amount to very little if the manager fails at their task. Such is the unignorable importance of managers. They operate in a position between the executives and regular employees, and must keep the company's wheels constant, in a fluid motion.

No one explains the gravity of the managerial position more clearly than Peter Drucker, who is celebrated as the leading thinker on this subject. He is famously quoted as saying, "The productivity of work is not the responsibility of the worker but of the manager." This means that if sales or team morale is going down, the manager's actions or inactions are likely responsible.

If you think management is a stressful place to be, you're right; it can be. The anxiety associated with this position can develop a person's escapist habits and even cause depression. This is why not everyone is a fit for the job. Being good at your job or consecutively voted employee of the month isn't enough to prepare someone for the responsibilities of management. To curb this anxiety, only those who enjoy the challenge of facing new tasks and managing both their strengths and weaknesses may ascend to this position and stay there. They should also be able to take the heat from the executives, without transferring undue aggression to their subordinates. Still, having these skills will not ensure success as a manager.

For new and experienced managers who seek knowledge on how to balance friendliness with professionalism, engage the members of their team, and boost productivity, this book is what you need. It is commendable that you want to learn more and retrain yourself in this field, especially if you are already a seasoned pro. So, go ahead and give yourself a well-deserved pat on the back.

Instead of following the well-worn path of performance ratings and strict developmental plans, this book attempts to enlighten you about morality and ethicality in management. These are often overlooked in favor of abstract and unfeeling numbers. But maintaining business etiquette, interacting with your teammates from a place of kindness, and a decent emotional intelligence are the secrets of lasting managerial success.

Keep reading to learn how to establish empathy and kindness as your principles, without compromising professionalism and productivity.

Chapter 1: Polish Your Managerial Dancing Shoes

A manager's role may include the recruitment of new staff, organizing employees, and relaying the wishes of top executives. They need to accomplish these tasks and more without alienating or losing the respect of those under their leadership. This means creating a perfect manager-employee relationship.

Workers who occupy non-leadership positions come in all personalities with different behavioral traits. While some seem endowed with all the proper work ethics, others need a little fine-tuning. You can't always rely on "sacking" someone because you can't fire someone solely for their lone wolf behavior. An employee could be perfect for the job, and not fit well into workplace culture or with the coworkers. It rests on the manager to diagnose where each employee is lacking and help them individually.

To achieve this, it is imperative that the manager reviews and espouses the culture of their company. For instance, they need to see you working smart which sometimes means working hard and always being kind. Next, you should teach this culture to your employees. Your team needs to move as one body. As the manager, you lead the dance, and your team should follow in smooth unison. The problem with this is that some managers attempt to direct their employees to the detriment of their individuality. They fall into the snare of a one-size-fits-all strategy and ignore the unique talents of each member.

What will immediately result from this is inconsistent performance from teammates. While some will excel and feel valued, many of your crew might be unproductive, anxious, and struggle with feelings of exclusion. Indeed, it takes some work to give the right amount of attention to each employee. As a manager, you should be able to move past your personal issues and be mentally and emotionally present for your team. This is the only way to notice and utilize their separate talents and potentials.

Some level of selflessness will be required for you to be an observant and empathic manager. You would need to care about the lives of every employee. Indeed, the manager can take on the role as parent, among others. Depending on the situation, you can be everything from a coach, student, and therapist to your workers.

You should be willing to fight for them and allow them to fight for you in turn. This is because your managerial position does not exactly change your humanity in one way or another. From a president managing their country to kindergarten teachers, everyone has their own struggles, flaws, and limitations. As such, managers should be willing to accept help. Self-control is another skill that is necessary to be a successful manager. You will be faced with trying personalities and crisis situations that demand a cool head to be properly handled. As a manager you cannot afford to let your anger or elation get out of control. Among other skills, you should work on showing only the parts of your personality that the occasion demands.

Now, you might read that and wonder if what is being described isn't pretentiousness. But managers are not encouraged to be phony. Instead, you should take a real interest in your workers and want them to succeed. What is at play here is a masterful blend of intuitiveness and empathy. The manager can be a coach one minute, and a student the next. Since your mood and energy filters through the team, you should be careful about how you affect them.

In different situations, you want to be assertive, patient, experienced, kind, and charismatic. The way you move from one character trait to the next is as important as how they are performed. You should be graceful and gradual, like the perfect waltz, more like a dimmer switch than an on/off button. If you switch carelessly between emotions and characters, your employees might get confused and feel less trust for the person in charge.

Characteristics of a Bad Manager

1. **Everything for personal gain:** The company's mission and ideals must always come before the ambitions of the manager. As simple as this is, people often lose sight of the collective goal and "look out for themselves." Selfishness and disloyalty are the hallmarks of a poor manager. If you occupy the office of a manager, you should be

reminded that your actions must continually be for the good of the company, before your interests.

2. **Taking undue credit:** This is an offshoot of the first point but may be considered worse than mere selfishness. Considering the large workload that a managerial role entails, it makes sense that they feel responsible for the success and failure of their team. This becomes an issue when the manager keeps praise to themselves and outwardly blames their teammates for any mishap. This behavior encourages the employees to be unashamedly disloyal, as they must feel disconnected from the company.

3. **No room for growth:** With a bad manager, there is no development of skill by any member of the team. Employees are frightened of creativity and independence. Even the slightest mistake is chastised, and every task must be done according to the vision of the manager. In this way, micromanagement limits the productivity of individual employees and the company's progress as a whole.

4. **Favoritism**: Jealousy as a theme in the workplace is one of the most destructive things a manager can allow to thrive. Often, this feeling is inspired by perceived partiality. Every employee must be managed equally. To fail at this is to ruin office camaraderie. Managers must take care that their preference for certain individuals does not influence the opportunities they give them.

5. **Trust issues:** It is the job of the manager to stir trust in their employees. Achieving this could pose some difficulty if the manager is suspicious of their team members. Usually, the focus of this distrust is on the abilities of their workers. Such managers will want to oversee each step of a project to ensure its quality. There are also cases where managers feel threatened by their juniors' expertise and skill, seeking out and magnifying otherwise inconsequential errors.

6. **No praise:** Even the toughest of us would like to be praised for putting their best effort and accomplishing a task. Some managers erroneously believe that verbally appreciating their employees might cause them to be lazy, instead of motivating them to be more creative and work harder/smarter. As such, they refrain from recognizing the "job well done". There are other reasons why managers might withhold praise. One of which is that they don't care enough to see their employees as more than just another ID card.

7. **No direction:** Managers often leave the room thinking they have communicated with their employees. But merely talking is different from successfully passing information. If your team members are to be aligned with the company's direction, then the manager needs to clearly communicate this direction. It also has to be realistic to ensure that the employees are not overwhelmed—this is not the same as challenging them, which is a good thing. If clarity is not achieved and realistic goals are not set, then there is no direction. Your team members will be confused, and projects will either be completed late or left unfinished.

8. **Haughtiness:** The responsibilities of organizational heads differs greatly from those of a secretary. Yet, the immutable fact remains that we are all human beings. This is one culture that, as a manager, you should consider establishing among your teammates—equality. Some managers consider themselves lords or something akin to divinity and alienate their employees. They lack the self-awareness to overcome their delusions of grandeur and, as a result, cannot distinguish opportunistic behavior from true loyalty. Good managers recognize the hopelessness of being an expert in every field. They cannot possibly have the answers and must be open to the input of their teammates. They learn to leverage the unique gifts of their employees.

9. **Unavailability**: In a bid to avoid dealing with conflicts or avoid the tough questions of their employees, some managers are often unreachable. They might intentionally present an attitude that scares people from approaching their doors or may be entirely unavailable. What often results from this is chaos, confusion, and disillusionment. As revealed by the American Management Association, conflict management is 24% of a manager's daily task (Le Phan, 2018). To ignore this fraction of your job portends a divided team and unproductiveness.

10. **Encouraging poor performance**: Giving chances to a weak teammate does not make a bad manager. It becomes a problem if they are persistently bad at their job. Keeping such an individual around will help neither the employee in question nor the team. It is a dangerous move to suffer mediocrity or downright incompetence. Your employees might consider you to be weak and doubt your leadership. It might also foster incompetence in skilled and hardworking team members.

11. **Does not practice what they preach**: This is one of the quickest ways to lose your employees respect. If you insist on certain moral conducts and office rules, the employees must see you openly practicing them.

Chapter 2: Kindness Is Key

"An ounce of pure kindness a day, can keep a pound of adversity away."

In today's fast-paced world filled with contrasting personalities and puzzling circumstances, it can be encouraging to realize that many of life's difficult questions are easily answered. Often, all it takes to manage a complicated situation is kindness. But, to fully appreciate what kindness is, we have to understand the nuances involved. For example, a smile is beautiful, but it does not paint a complete picture of what it means to be kind. The same applies to being nice or doing good deeds.

Although these behaviors (kindness, smiling, pleasantness, and good deeds) share some similarities, it is important that they are not confused or mean the same thing. The quality of being nice could be compared to pleasantness. It does not take into account the intentions of the doer. Niceness is ephemeral and may be pretentious or hypocritical. The chances that nice actions will be repeated are usually terribly low. Kind deeds are helpful, considerate, compassionate, and edifying. This is when pleasantness, good deeds, a welcoming demeanor, and genuine selflessness all coincide.

This further drives home the necessity of practicing self-awareness. Only those who are conscious of their actions and the motivation behind them will be able to correctly separate mere niceness from actual kindness. And, as a result, they can work on being even kinder to themselves and others. More than most people, managers need to be self-aware. For instance, pardoning consistent slip-ups by an employee may be seen as kind by external observers. But, in truth, you are not doing neither employee nor the company any favors by not firmly addressing the issue. Offering superficial praise in an attempt to gain the approval of your employees can not be characterized as kindness.

The Importance of Kindness

Now that we know how kindness differs from being nice, managers must understand why they must continually choose to be kind each day. Regardless of the people you interact with, or how annoying a particular situation is, you need to rein in the urge to lash out and only respond with kindness. Below are a few reasons why.

1. To reiterate a previous fact, managers need to embody whatever principles and ideologies they are vocal about. They must lead by example. The same applies to kindness. If you want to cultivate kind acts as the norm among your teammates, it needs to start with you. Thankfully, this behavior is quite contagious. If you are unfailingly compassionate, your employees will be spurred to treat themselves with the same consideration.
2. Being truly kind to your employees gives you a hit of dopamine that boosts your happiness level. This is not a fleeting emotion either. Dopamine is the same chemical that causes mothers to bond with their children. This means that the more kind actions you perform, the greater the bond and loyalty between you and your team members.

3. Managers are not exempt from feelings of dissatisfaction. They might feel stressed and incapable of deriving joy from their jobs. Showing kindness is a great way to destress, and research has shown to improve mental health and allow for an increased enjoyment in tasks (Stevenson, 2018). By being kind and seeing the result of such an act, we learn that we are not alone in the trials of life

Ways to Show Kindness

1. Never walk past your employees without greeting them or responding to their salutations. If you can, inquire about their wellbeing and wait for a reply. Verbally appreciating their efforts at work or when they do you a favor is equally as important. This level of friendship applies if you meet your team members physically at work, outside work, or during a virtual meeting.
2. As well trained as an employee might be, they could be lacking in a particular skill or knowledge. This is especially true for new employees. Be willing to spend time teaching them things like new software or amended company policies. This should, of course, be done when you are not busy with other more crucial tasks.
3. Seek out an employee who you haven't touched base with for a while and reach out. Do them a favor, engage in small talk, or treat them to midday lunch. Try not to overdo it with displays of kindness, but find a good balance of friendliness and professionalism.
4. Remember the birthdays of your employees. Depending on the size of your team, this could prove difficult or be easy. Either way, you should

make an effort to celebrate your employee's birthdays in simple yet meaningful ways.

5. Constructive feedback can also be an act of kindness. Criticism comes easily to most managers. But those conversations might be the perfect time to foster trust with your team. You will not be perceived as a weak manager for delivering feedback with kindness. It just makes your words less abrasive and more encouraging. You can follow these steps to be candid with your employees without seeming hostile.

a.   Do not start by stating the problem. First, let the team member know *why* you are giving this feedback. You can also take time to voice appreciation for the areas in which they excel.

b.   Explain *what* the problem is. Endeavor to do this without being judgmental. Simply describe the issue from your perspective and let them know its effects on the company and other team members.

c.   Next, *listen* as the employee explains things from their own point of view. You can tell a lot in this step. For instance, does the employee take responsibility for their mistakes, or are they needlessly defensive. You can gain some clarity on the problem by just listening.

d.   Finally, it's time to move past the issue. Proffer solutions at this point and encourage them to do better.

With these points as a guide, can you list any acts of kindness you have performed today? They needn't be something grand or even office related. The simplest gestures, when done with sincerity, can be quite meaningful. Did you patiently listen to a friend? Did you offer kind words to a brokenhearted colleague? It should take no more than a few minutes to quickly list out ten kind acts you have performed today. Don't fret if you cannot think of this many. Even one might be more impactful than you realize.

Chapter 3: Know Your Style

Management style refers to how they organize subordinates for maximum growth and productivity. This includes the various techniques and methodologies that could be engaged for the unique structure of different companies. The size of the workforce and what industry the business is a part are some factors that determine the management style to be employed.

In many cases, management styles emanate from an individual's personality and outlook on life. They lead their team members based on their ideologies and principles, and this often becomes quite problematic. Your chosen style of management should not be comparable to governmental laws, which are based on generalizations. It is also inadvisable to direct people of varying backgrounds, strengths, and weaknesses like you would yourself.

Instead, your management style should be formed around its unique work environment and culture. Social views on which style is the most productive must be excluded from your decision. They are often biased and would likely not fit your particular company anyway. Managers usually factor in the industry's nature when choosing which management style would produce the best result. But even that presents the same problem as social views and individual personality as a decision-maker.

Instead, narrow your focus only to include things like the culture and size of your team. Your style of management should positively impact each employee and lead to overall growth.

The Importance of Knowing Your Style

If having a distinct management style seems like too much trouble, you might decide just to wing it. There are a few problems with this choice, and they are listed below.

1. Like dieting and fashion, new techniques for managing employees pop up every time. There will always be an "improved" method that is "guarantee" to organize your team members for optimum productivity. But these are often little more than fads. They disappear almost as soon as some internet management guru introduces them. As such, you need to pattern, for yourself, a management style and stick to it. Otherwise, you might end up with confused employees who are frequently presented with a "new" manager.

2. By settling on a management style that fits your company's goals and culture, you can easily adapt to new challenges. You will be able to deal consistently with the suddenness and nuances of various work emergencies—be it strategizing or overdue deadlines.

3. It is also easier to work on self-development when you have a consistent style of management. This is because different rules and skills apply to the various systems available. Your commitment to a single style allows you to identify areas of weakness and work on them effortlessly.

4. Effectively and productively engaged employees are less likely to jump ship. Regardless of the nature of the job, most people just want to be a significant part of the business and compensated for their efforts adequately. Sticking to a management style encourages your employees to approach you with any new ideas or questions. It also helps you learn

about your team members and how best to engage their expertise.

Types of Management Styles

In general, management styles usually belong to four categories. These are the consultative, autocratic, participative, and persuasive approach. From their names, you might be able to guess at the nature of these general styles. The autocratic approach makes little room for questioning by the employees, and they are to promptly follow the commands of the manager. The consultative style is the polar opposite of autocracy, as the employees are encouraged to share their opinions. The participative style takes consultation a step further by urging each employee to give their suggestions, and run with them. For the persuasive approach, team members are explained why the higher-ups have chosen a particular direction, instead of simply commanding them to act.

None of these approaches are without their benefits and drawbacks. While teams are not built in an autocracy, it might be perfect for crisis situations. The manager must decide on the right approach for the challenge they are faced with.

Now, let's discuss the management styles that can be utilized for success in business.

Authoritative Style

This isn't always encouraged as a suitable management technique, but there are a few situations that call for office dictatorship. If your previous management model is faulty, this could lead to a chaotic situation that demands drastic action. You might also be new to your role as a manager and presented with disorganization or lack of structure. It might be difficult trying to gain the respect and attention of your subordinates by choosing a democratic approach.

Some managers wrongly assume that the authoritative management style is a license to be rude. They might come up with a host of extreme punishments for the misbehavior of their employees. Such an attitude to management completely defeats the purpose of shaping up your employees and making them more productive. Instead, you will end up with grungy workers who despise their boss and derive no pleasure from their jobs.

Managers must be reminded that the authoritative style does not work if it is merely a projection of their aggressive personalities. Again, this management style should only be used under certain conditions. For instance, your team members might be inexperienced at a time when the company needs huge profits. In this scenario, a dictatorship is understandable for high performance in a short time. You should stay away from the authoritative style if your employees are more experienced or self-starters.

Democratic Style

For managers who have an experienced team and trust in their employees abilities, democracy is often the more useful technique. With this management style, you allow your workers to contribute to the company's growth, as opposed to merely running errands. The democratic manager remains present and active in the decision making process. But they entertain the ideas of every team member and display confidence in their judgment.

They might consult the expertise of their subordinates, instead of barking orders. Frequently, the democratic manager is also a motivational leader. This means they are genuinely interested in their team members growth and have the charisma and patience to help them achieve just that. These managers might be willing to lend an ear and more than a few kind words to their teammates, even after office hours. In some cases, a manager might solicit their employees' opinion on vital issues involving company policies. Such is the level of collaboration that could exist in a democratic style of management.

The democratic manager also sets the bar with their deeds. They give rules to their subordinates and live by them too. These managers do not mind rolling up their sleeves. Their employees can learn the right way to conduct themselves by watching them.

Result-Based Style

This works best for managers, who care very little about the process it takes to achieve a certain result. They are more interested in efficient and productive workers than any ideology or principle. These managers may also prioritize speed over the quality of work delivered. As disadvantageous as this seems, there are a few benefits to being a result-oriented manager. If you are faced with the challenge of meeting multiple deadlines, it is sensible to be less bothered about processes.

This technique also spurs leaders to make company policy and managerial changes when an employee presents a more effective method of achieving the same goals.

Laissez-Faire Style

This is for the laid-back manager who also happens to have a well-trained team. They can give their team members more leeway to make crucial decisions. For this to work, the manager should not be lazy. People are often able to tell laziness from the delegation, and you do not want to lose the respect of your employees. The fact that you do not micromanage your employees is no excuse to be absent.

The Laissez-Faire style allows managers to function as coaches, rather than bosses. If your employees are highly trained and fully understand your company's structure, processes, and goals, you can step back and act as a mentor for even higher productiveness.

Affiliative Style

This style is participative and seeks to make allies out of employees. Instead of looking down from their position as managers, leaders who choose this style make themselves almost indistinguishable from the rest of the team. They are always available to help and ease the workload of their teammates. This technique is great for creating a harmonious and loyal team. Yet, care needs to be taken that mediocrity or disrespect is not promoted.

There are more styles of management than what has been covered in this chapter. You may have designed one that is peculiar to your company. Whichever method you incorporate, there are general rules that must be maintained.

You must be mindful of going to the extreme with your management style. Whether you choose to be friendly or strict, never compromise on ethicality. Also, ensure that your style of management is not a reflection of your personality. While empathy is laudable, it is inadvisable to be emotional about your decisions as a manager.

This final part is an opportunity to review your management technique. Which style do you subscribe to, and why have you chosen it? Your honesty and thoroughness are important in this section. Use the space below to detail this. Next, carefully analyze what you have written. With the knowledge gained from this chapter as a guide, are you comfortable with your management style? Is it a self-serving style, or does it benefit the goals of your company? Does it promote independence among your team members, or is it micromanaging? If you think your style might need some tweaking, do not be hesitant to do so.

Chapter 4: Emotional Intelligence

Like its more popular counterpart, IQ, every human being is born with some degree of emotional intelligence (EQ or EI). In childhood, we usually exhibit various forms of EQ, including empathy and social skills. However, the familial and societal environment in which we are raised shapes our perception of and interaction with the world. And, as a result, we might grow or decrease in emotional intelligence.

Scientists such as John D. Mayer, Peter Salovey, and Daniel Goleman have, since the 90s, preached about the significance of a high EQ to success in leadership. In fact, they placed it tiers above IQ in its relevance to CEOs, managers, teachers, parents, and politicians. In recent times, business leaders like Gary Vaynerchuk, who embody EQ qualities, do not take a break from talking about the health, relationship, and productivity benefits of increasing one's emotional intelligence. Hence, this book would not be complete without discussing how developing your EQ will make you a better manager.

The History of Emotional Intelligence

Even before the 1990s, when the discussion and study of emotional intelligence gained traction and popularity, there has always been some interest in the concept, but it did not go by the same name. There is an unmistakable similarity between social intelligence and the more recent terminology, EQ. In the 1930s, Edward Thorndike studied the social skills of human beings and how they can be improved. About a decade later, David Wechsler revealed the forms of social intelligence that could be employed to achieve even greater success in relationships and business.

In the years to come, these concepts will enjoy further developments by some of the most brilliant minds in psychology and philosophy. The year 1943 saw Abraham Maslow come up with his Hierarchy of Needs. This theory posited that among the five most potent desires of every human being, self-actualization—the drive to achieve our highest potential—is the greatest. Generally, Maslow encouraged the pursuit of emotional growth as an evolution of the debate on EQ. The theory of multiple intelligences was another defining moment, as Howard Gardner linked both psychometric and emotional perspectives to this. Gardner did not limit his study to only these two types. In total, he defined eight types of intelligence. They include musical, linguistic-verbal, visual-spatial, naturalistic, logical-mathematical, bodily-kinesthetic, intrapersonal, and interpersonal intelligence. Gardner also suggested the likelihood of existentialist data to prove that one could not conclude on an individual's lack of intelligence by observing a single aspect.

Until the 1980s, people talked about emotional intelligence in the broad sense of social intelligence or the separate lights of interpersonal and intrapersonal intelligences.

Wayne Payne coined the term Emotional Intelligence (EI) in 1985, and in 1987, Keith Beasley introduced the Emotional Quotient (EQ). We mustn't forget the groundbreaking, 1990 article written by Peter Salovey and John Mayer. This article presented EI as one's ability to interpret other's feelings as well as their own, and use this information to guide actions.

Still, the concept did not become as commonly known and accepted until 1995 when Daniel Goleman wrote the book *Emotional Intelligence: Why It Can Matter More Than IQ*. After this, public interest concerning the subject surged. More people have taken an interest in EQ and now engage their peers in meaningful conversations regarding the benefits and steps to improve their emotional intelligence.

What Is Emotional Intelligence?

To be considered emotionally intelligent, one must display an understanding of their own emotions and those of the people they interact with. They should also be able to manage these emotions. As such, words like self-awareness, introspection, self-control, and empathy are frequently used in the discussion about EQ. The development of this type of intelligence forces us to take a step back from the rush and selfishness that categorizes the present fourth industrial revolution. As a result of the control afforded by high emotional intelligence, it is no wonder that managers who develop this part of their character can lead their team towards harmony and productivity. Who wouldn't thrive under the leadership of a boss who is relatable and always appears calm, even in stressful situations?

Daniel Goleman gave us a more comprehensive perspective on emotional intelligence. He also summarized the various components of the concept into five elements. They include empathy, self-awareness, self-regulation, social skills, and motivation.

Empathy

This is a person's ability to feel the pain and distress and another person. You may never be able to completely relate to someone else's stress, grief, or physical pain. However, empathy brings you closer to the feelings and emotions of people around you.

Merely recognizing these feelings is not sufficient to describe empathy. You should be able and willing to use this new perspective in dealing with the person you are trying to help. Do they need a kind word or your quiet presence? Should you be gentle or do something exciting to boost their spirits? Such are the questions that empathy encourages you to ask and answer.

You can also be empathetic towards more than individuals. Managers who have adequately developed this skill can sense and influence the dynamics of their team and company in general. These folks are able to figure out the minority who influence the behaviors, emotions and, as a consequence, culture of the work environment as well as detect manipulation.

Types of Empathy

1. **Cognitive empathy**: This has less to do with emotions, and is a lot more involved with figuring out the thoughts of their conversation partner. You are still trying to view things from the eye of the other person, but this time, you want to learn what they must be thinking instead of what they must be feeling. For instance, you might have an employee who is quite competent but is now distressed by not completing a certain task. With cognitive empathy, you can recognize how capable the employee is and their need to meet the leader's expectations. You can also estimate the thought processes that ensue from failing, especially if they are perfectionists or live somewhere with a high unemployment rate.
2. **Affective empathy:** This is the more commonly known form of empathy. To display this type of intelligence, you would have to open yourself to be *affected* by emotions other than yours. And it is possible to be successfully empathetic in this way without the prior experience of certain emotions. For example, you can put yourself in the proverbial shoes of a grieving team member, even though you have not suffered the loss of a loved one.
3. **Somatic empathy:** This is a physical and noticeable response that mirrors the feelings of other people. Think of the times you yawned because you saw someone else doing the same thing. If you have ever blushed or cringed as a reaction to embarrassing actions by someone else, then you have displayed somatic empathy.

Self-Awareness

This could be described as internalized empathy. As certain as you might be about your emotions and their impact on those close to you, your understanding may not be as close to the facts as you think. To improve self-awareness, you should catch your various emotions and track their influence over your life and that of others. Often, what we believe are knee-jerk reactions stem from feelings we fail to control or entirely ignore.

Self-aware people recognize which feelings impact their behavior and choices the most. They can also tell the perception of themselves that is projected. This is an important skill for managers whose power lies mostly in the way they are perceived. You want to be seen as a strong yet approachable leader. Self-awareness allows you to reveal if you are winning at this or not. By looking inwards with honesty and humility, you can learn your weaknesses and strengths. You must remember that neither self-hatred nor self-flagellation is the goal of this exercise. Instead, you should appreciate your flaws as well as your beauty and proficiencies. The emotional maturity afforded by such a mindset will greatly improve your confidence, sense, and relationship with others.

It should be noted that self-awareness is dissimilar to self-consciousness. The latter is not beneficial to emotional growth, and may even set you back. Self-conscious people are perpetually, and painfully, aware of themselves in every situation. They may be observed showing signs of anxiety and are often reluctant to try new things. None of that fits the scope of emotional intelligence. Unsure managers are often incapable of commanding the followership and respect of their employees.

How Self-Awareness Develops

Self-awareness grants you the wisdom to navigate various difficult situations as a distinct personality. To some degree, everyone is self-aware. Even understanding that one is separate from the rest of the world can also be described as awareness of self. While it may surprise you, newborns and infants display a level of self-awareness, and this was proven in a fairly recent study published by Science Direct. We learn from the study that a newborn's ability to tell when they are being touched by someone else (non self-touch) from when *they* touch themselves (self-touch) is a solid example of basic self-awareness (Rochat, 2003). Infants also show the same understanding as they reach for a nipple when they feel an external object on their faces.

At about a year old, we begin to mature in this awareness. To prove this more complex sense of self, Brooks-Gunn and Lewis performed a simple, yet adequate experiment. They made a red mark on the noses of infants below, at, or above the age of one. These children were then placed before a mirror. If they touched the mark on their face by looking at the mirror, this was considered sufficient proof for basic self-awareness. A negligible number of kids who were younger than one year old touched the mark on their face. This number went up to 25% for 18-month old kids and 70% for infants who were about two years old (Brooks-Gunn & Lewis, 1984).

Today, we do not conclude that the experiment above is definitive for proving the level of self-awareness in children. Standing before a mirror and identifying one's self is a display of visual self-awareness alone. There is a variety of awareness and, when all studied, the numbers rise considerably. For instance, some infants are better at expressing emotions than identifying their images in a mirror. And to express emotions, one must see themselves as distinct and in relation to the people and objects around them. That is, children may not express their desire to be carried and moved around if they cannot see themselves as separate entities.

While you, as the manager, are expected to show more than a sense of individuality, that is a good place to start from— the recognition and appreciation of all the things that make you different.

Types of Self-Awareness

1. **Private awareness**. It is hidden because it is not felt or expressed to anyone else. Kids recognizing their reflection is a good example of this kind of self-awareness. The unsettling feeling in your stomach when you forgot an almost overdue deadline is another way we express private awareness.
2. **Public awareness.** This is when we recognize how we appear to other people. It is a beneficial product of social evolution, as we are made to act for the good of our group when we perceive that we are being examined. To avoid getting kicked out of our tribe, we present behaviors that are acceptable and desirable. As one might have figured out, public self-awareness can quickly escalate to heightened self-consciousness. At this point, it is no longer beneficial, and it might be wise for the individual to leave the distressing environment.

Motivation

This is not the buzz of excitement from watching inspirational videos on the internet. While these motivational aids have relevance, one should use them to seek and develop the drive that is provided by self-awareness. There are two types of motivation. One is intrinsic, and this is the less common but emotionally intelligent kind. It is when individuals, for internal rewards, inspire themselves to behave in certain ways. To illustrate this, think of managers who allow their employees the independence to make choices and contribute to the company, for the singular satisfaction of seeing them grow. If you are spurred by extrinsic motivation, you either seek external rewards in kind or cash, or just want to avoid negative consequences.

Although many of us act on extrinsic motivation, the reward is not as gratifying. The more often you enforce an action based on external rewards, the less intrinsically motivated they become. This is termed the overjustification effect. If, for instance, students are rewarded with gifts for every course they pass, they would gradually become less passionate about their academic pursuits. Overjustification also affects professionals like managers. If taken by the praise and bonuses they get for leading their team, managers might lose their true motivation for seeing their team members grow.

The reliance on external rewards also hinders the flow of creativity. If one engages in a task for the love of it, they would be more likely to figure out new and effective ways of getting it done. The motivation that comes from self-awareness and self-realization often causes individuals to persevere through a challenge and find creative and novel solutions. If their passion were hinged on gratitude and other external rewards, they would only be concerned with seeing the task to completion. In such situations, there is very little pride or satisfaction that can be gotten from the project or activity itself. Instead, the individual would merely look forward to the external rewards.

Some Factors That Spark Intrinsic Motivation

1. **Control**: If asked about their career choice, people might claim it was solely driven by passion. While there is some truth to this, the true motivation is often the need to maintain control over their lives. Most people give their best to a task, driven by the belief that their actions determine their destiny.
2. **Acclaim**: To address what you are probably thinking right now: no, this is not a contradiction. Although getting recognition and appreciation for your input are examples of external rewards, they can be beneficial to intrinsic motivation. If you understand that your internal rewards were responsible for your success, the acclaim that comes after may encourage you to look even further inwards for motivation.
3. **Challenge**: You can envision yourself crossing a hurdle and fueled by the desire to realize this goal. There is often a direct correlation between intrinsic motivation and self-esteem. Win or lose, people can gain respect for themselves solely because they tried to reach a goal or conquer a challenge.
4. **Cooperation**: There is usually an undeniable delight and fulfillment that comes in the wake of doing a good deed for someone else. This emotion can be heightened in a collaborative environment. There is nothing wrong with returning favors, healthy competition, and cooperation. However,

things can take a negative turn if any team member begins to keep a score of favors or good deeds.

Self-Regulation

After improving your empathetic and self-awareness skills, you must also learn to control the emotions you are presented with. It means that you shouldn't try to read other's emotions or monitor your own feelings and projected personality all the time. Conversely, it would be unwise to turn away from these emotions. You just need to know when to turn off empathy and be self-aware. With enough experience, self-regulation will endow you with adaptability skills. Indeed, all the benefits of emotional intelligence are unlocked after one can regulate their emotions.

It might be surprising to know that self-regulation doesn't need to be a skill we develop as adults. Typically, infants well catered to, find it easy to manage their emotions. The problem begins when parents neglect the basic needs of their still helpless children. It was revealed in a study that this bad parenting gives rise to fear and distrust in an infant's mind, and it grows with them to manifest as a lack of self-regulation and poor emotional intelligence (Spratt, et al., 2012). Now adults and not equipped with the strategies to handle tough emotions and trying situations might succumb to depression and harmful vices.

Although termed self-regulation, learning this skill will force you to take responsibility for your influence over other people's actions. One of the best situations to observe such an impact is the relationship between managers and their employees. You may find it quite easy to blame mishaps on your team members' incompetence while ignoring your faults. By regulating your feelings and actions, you know when to take responsibility for your involvement. Also individuals who practice self-regulation are often extremely conscientious. For example, self-regulated students find it easier to motivate themselves to study for a test.

Admittedly, the ability to pause and think before acting does not come easy to most people. Everyone, from children to adults, struggle with reining in their feelings and considering the pros and cons of a particular course of action. That said, it is far from an impossible task. And after considering the personal and professional rewards involved, you would realize that this exercise is worth the time and energy.

One of the biggest advantages of this skill is how it lets you behave in line with your principles and values. Both negative and positive emotions can be so powerful that they make us act in ways that do not correctly portray who we are. With self-regulation, you can mindfully express yourself without damaging the way you are perceived. Managers can act with kindness, even during chaotic situations.

Tips for Improving Self-Regulation

1. **Cognitive reappraisal**: When faced with challenges or disappointment, the first line of thought might be to look at the negative angle of the situation. If, for instance, a loved one denies your request, you might conclude that this must mean they do not love you the same. Yet, you hold the power to reframe your mind and think about the situation in a more positive light. To keep with the example above, you could reinterpret the denial to

mean that the loved one truly *cannot* meet your request, they were busy, or you did not clearly explain your predicament. When you reappraise your thought processes, you prevent yourself from needlessly vilifying people or burning bridges.

2. **Mindfulness**: This is characterized by the presence of mind and purposeful actions. Most times, those two factors are absent in our dealings with people. We make false conclusions based on emotions or judge people based on their past behavior. To be mindful, one must work on being attentive, regardless of the nature of the situation. Even though we feel like cutting people off our lives, punishing them, or using harsh words against those we feel have intentionally hurt us, it is important to always give them a chance to prove you wrong. To effectively navigate stressful and emotionally charged conversations, breathe with intention and be highly cautious not to say or do anything you will regret. This might seem like a basic concept, but it will distract your mind long enough for you to cool down and consider a different perspective. With this practice you might find you are more grateful for all of the good things an individual has done for you in the past.

Social Skills

As a manager, all the other components of EQ lead up to the way you deal with people. Whether they are your bosses or subordinates, you should juggle the necessary social interactions with dexterity. It is no wonder that the study of social intelligence predates all the other parts of emotional intelligence. This is because our failure in this regard (which often) is usually the most impactful. Our verbal and non-verbal communication with people affects more than just our lives. The happiness and productivity of the other person are also at stake. If you hope to build symbiotic relationships with company heads and team members, it is important to develop social intelligence.

Traits of Social Intelligence

1. We all know someone who seems to get in and out of conversations with ease. Everybody welcomes their presence and input. They can be serious, funny, and transparent just when they need to be. These are the individuals to emulate as you build your social skills.
2. Another way to identify a person with good social skills is to remember important details about their conversation partners. Merely committing the name of your employee to memory goes a long way in warming them towards you. It communicates the fact that you now see them as more than another addition to the workforce.
3. In any social interaction, people want to feel understood and appreciated. And there is no better way to accomplish this than by actively listening. One advantage of paying attention in this way is the opportunity to learn even more about people. Since we also need to be listened to, the second benefit comes when employees, leaders, friends, and family members return the favor.
4. While it is undoubtedly tricky, socially intelligent individuals know how to maintain a sparkling reputation, without ever being inauthentic, this means that even though you are careful with your actions, you never want to confuse your team

members by seeming distant or "off." Maintaining this balance is the product of a commitment to improving one's social intelligence. It might take a while, but you will eventually learn to manage your reputation and seem familiar.

5. Although it is not entirely impossible to find socially intelligent people arguing, it is a rare occurrence. Again, reputation is everything to these sets of people, and they don't want to be known as individuals who reject opposing ideas. To improve your social skills, you would have to approach the opinions of others with open minds. Also, very little is achieved in a shouting match. While you might think that raising your voice will change the other person's mind while in an argument, this is usually not the case.

Developing Social Skills

1. As stated earlier, you must build the other components of emotional intelligence—motivation, empathy, self-awareness, and self-regulation—before moving on to social skills. Redundant as this might seem, the first four parts of EQ reveal your true self to you. By practicing them, you are endowed with the ability to predict your actions more accurately. Only after you have figured yourself out, can you maneuver the turbulence of negative feelings and excitement in social situations.

2. Cultivate meaningful relationships with your loved ones. Even though this book is primarily about the manager-employee relationship, you can gain the necessary experience by tending to your relationship with your kids, spouse, and other close friends or family members. Some of the social skills

to practice here include attentiveness to their emotions and patience.

3. Be observant. At first, you should pay more attention to those you exhibit the traits of high social intelligence. Notice how they interact with people, and try to emulate this aspect of their character. Also, observe those who seem to have poor social skills and their actions that inform this perception. If you can figure out what they do wrong, you would be able to avoid making the same mistakes. The observational skills of a manager can be useful in helping them influence workplace culture in a positive way.

4. One of the reasons why we react differently to the same situations is because of our upbringing. Culture plays a defining role in our character. As such, socially intelligent managers strive to understand the cultural diversity among their employees. This would inform how you interact with each one of them, and the behaviors you would expect.

5. Many conversations involve one party waiting for the other to finish speaking, just so they can voice their thoughts. This wait doesn't always mean listening. If you improve your social skills, you will be more attentive when anyone is speaking with you. This means that you not only hear the words but the meaning and feelings behind them. It is also important that you think about the words you just heard before responding. This is defined as active listening.

You would have to put aside such distractions as your phone or laptop, and focus on the person conversing with you. By practicing this skill, you'll be guided by even the inflections on words and non-verbal communication.

Chapter 5: Golden Rules for Business Etiquette

"Do unto others as you would have them do unto you."

Isn't a company just a smaller, more compact version of the world? We make friends out of colleagues, and these people eventually become part of our families. There are also rules, hierarchy, and a diversity of personalities and abilities. For smooth operation of the system, there needs to be in place a code of conduct that promotes camaraderie. Each employee must understand that they can only make progress by looking out for the success of their teammates. The question is: How does a manager establish proper business etiquette?

1. **Lead by example.** The mutual respect and love that keeps the world from coming undone need to be applied. And the manager must be the first to openly display this attitude. You may have heard the saying "do as I say, not as I do." As a manager trying to foster trust and team spirit among your employees, you cannot afford to be this discreditable. Your actions need to be a glowing example of how employees should behave—and this should come before any lectures on proper conduct.

   In the modern work environment, much of what is known as organizational bureaucracy has already been dismantled. Instead of getting blocked by hierarchy, a line staff can directly contact executives as well as the CEO. While the chain of command is still necessary and encouraged for the sake of order, the manager cannot hide behind bureaucracy and be unprincipled. This transparency means that managers must teach their employees to learn from their actions as well as their words.

2.   **Watch what you say.** Words can make or mar people and relationships. You create a perception of yourself in your team member's minds by your choice of words and how you verbally express your opinions. Employees often lose or gain respect for their managers after listening to them speak. This isn't to say that you must have a pre-written speech before every meeting. It just means that, if your job involves managing people, you need to train yourself to handle words carefully.

3.   **Dress the part.** It is not expected that managers should have stylists on hand and only wear luxury outfits. It is enough that your clothes are appropriate for work and they are clean and undamaged. Appearance communicates a lot about character and self-image. You would put in the effort to look your best on a date. Usually because you want the admiration and respect of your partner. Coming to work in overly worn clothes portrays a lack of professionalism and mediocrity. Also, there is no better way to teach your employees to take pride in their appearance than by dressing the part each day no matter how you feel.

4.   **Your management style**. The way you organize and direct your team plays a major role in determining how your employees will interact with themselves. As mentioned earlier, an autocratic style does not promote teamwork. Your employees will see each other as just another cog in the wheel vigorously, but almost mindlessly, trying to make it through the day. If you are extremely laid-back, your team members might begin to cross each other's boundaries and not take their jobs seriously. Having read chapter three, you may have already decided on a method. It merits a second mention because of how dependent business etiquette is on management style.

5.   **Changing your management style.** If there is anything more important than maintaining your style, it is being able to change it without shocking or confusing your employees. After reading the chapter on management style, you might have decided to do things differently. To spare your team members the disillusionment of meeting a different boss and learning a new system, you should ease them into it. Do not prevent employees from resisting change. There is an advantage in communicating your reasons for the new style and it is more likely to ensure stability.

6.   **Confidence.** While boastfulness is not a virtue, managers should not downplay their achievements and expertise. You can display self-confidence without seeming arrogant. If you choose to be silent about your successes or walk with your shoulders slumped, you cannot blame any employee for thinking less of you. In addition, your accomplishment can be a source of motivation for those who work alongside you. Those who aspire to occupy the same office as you someday need to know the hard work that led to your success.

7.   **Appreciate the various personalities**. Our individuality can be seen in everything from our fingerprints to personality traits. Managers have to deal with people of varying beliefs, histories, and behaviors. To manage them successfully, you must recognize the value that each team member brings to the company. Good managers can leverage the strengths of each employee and give each one adequate responsibility. As a result, the whole team thrives.

8.   **Stability is key.** The rate of unemployment in many countries is so high many people are overwhelmed by the possibility of losing their jobs. Part of your duty as a manager is to alleviate fears as best you can. The company needs to have a well-defined and constant *modus operandi* or mode of operating. Managers should be careful about changing the rate at which they hire or reduce staff. The company's vision and agenda must also be clearly communicated to the employees. In gaining consensus, you would also have the trust of your teammates.

9.   **Create an environment for growth.** The goals of the modern employee do not stop at pleasing the boss and getting a promotion. People also seek professional development. Instead of routine activities, employees seek the opportunity to apply their knowledge and contribute creatively. Managers need to provide the resources and environment for their team members to shine. To overlook this might cause smart and enthusiastic workers to resign.

10.   **Positivity is key.** Regardless of the current work climate, managers need to consistently project optimism. Although it is advisable to look at life from a realistic standpoint, every issue will seem impossible if some confidence is not applied. Employees look to their leaders for direction. As such, the words and body language of managers must be positive and one of open-mindedness. Never resort to negativity as a defense mechanism when dealing with challenging situations. Soon the entire team will be affected by this culture of optimism.

> Now, we know people are more likely to chatter on about a negative event than a positive one. For this reason, pessimism tends to be more prominent in organizations than the bright side or route of positive thinking. As the manager, you must find a way to vent the negative energy. Otherwise, your employees might become victims of your pessimistic mindset. Think of it as the exhaust pipe in cars and similar machinery. They would soon stop working if those channels for letting out the by-products were not designed. Similarly, you need to find an outlet. For some, this is in the form of exercise, meditation, karaoke, etc.

11.   **Be honest**. Having chosen to employ an individual, you cannot proceed to treat them as unintelligent. To conclude that a team member is stupid because of their lack of enthusiasm is lazy on the part of the manager. The correct attitude is to approach the employee and have a discussion with them. Be willing to listen and carefully offer advice. If done right, you might help the employee be less withdrawn and make friends in the process.

12.   **Avoid using manipulation.** Some managers are known to apply manipulative techniques to keep their workers in line. This might appear to work for a while, but such methods are eventually revealed for what they are. The actual cost of blaming, guilt-tripping, intimidating, gaslighting, or shaming your teammates is never worth the expected rewards. Consider some of the disadvantages of manipulation below.

a.   You will be found out. And it doesn't matter how long you pull off the sneaky or deceitful behavior. Soon, your team members will figure out the disingenuity and be less trusting of you. This might escalate to a battle of wits, and very little productivity can be achieved after that.

b.   Except for sociopaths, the results of manipulation are never as satisfying as you would expect. You will be constantly reminded of the fact that the obedience and loyalty of your employees were ill-gotten. While your workers might show their confidence and trust in your leadership, you will remain suspicious of their true opinions.

c.   Manipulation also leads to unfair and unfounded assumptions. It is an addictive technique that causes the user to be deceitful before learning the truth.

> Some might argue that manipulation is necessary, and there is some truth to that. Manipulation *can* be used positively to enhance performance. And, on a subconscious level, we manipulate those we interact with almost every day. The important thing is that you are more honest than scheming.

13.   **Be respectful.** You may have heard the saying that people can more accurately recall how an experience made them feel than the actual situation. It may sound cliché, but it is unarguably true. Everyone, irrespective of the role they play in the company, deserves respect. Merely talking about mutual respect during meetings is not enough. You should also go out of your way to show it in an honest way.

14.   **Speak highly of your employees.** No successful company has ever been built on the input of just the managers or top executives. Although we rarely know the

names of the more populous line staff, their skill and diligence are invaluable contributions to the growth of any business. This is why you should not hesitate to showcase the achievements and abilities of your team members. Speak proudly of them.

15. **Know your people.** Until now, we have discussed the responsibilities of the manager as involving their subordinates. However, they are also required to look out for the interests of other company leaders, board members, shareholders, and customers. The titular *dance* is properly executed when managers can engage the human resources in their care towards the actualization of the leaders' vision, without compromising on the company culture and ideology. They are to engage their team to make a profit and provide the best possible value. To achieve this feat, they must know the various pieces at play. After all, it is near impossible to dance in time to a song you don't know. As such, the manager should figure out the demands, interests, and expectations of everyone they manage or answer to.

16. **Be an advocate.** As an extension of the point above, it is not out of place for managers to advocate on behalf of their employees. Your unique position makes you a liaison between the organizational heads and members of your team. Occasionally, some new policies and company procedures would be put forward by the leaders. If these changes would be detrimental to ordinary workers, be their voice to the executive and stakeholders. Of course, this should be done in a manner that would not put your job at risk. With wisdom and diplomacy, speak up for fairness.

17. **Work smart.** Contrary to some popular opinions, smart work does not negate hard work. However, working smart *is* an improvement on the idea that one must hustle for 15 hours every day to be wealthy or generally successful. You must plan out your day and tasks ahead of time. Even a temporary loss of leadership might have negative consequences on team focus and productivity as a result of the manager's burnout or mental breakdown. The next chapter of this book is devoted to outlining the benefits of smart work and practical steps on how to go about it.

18. **Learn and grow**. A manager who cares might hope that each member of their team grows significantly in

the shortest possible time. This growth, however, isn't only necessary for employees. Managers must continually educate themselves and grow both personally and professionally. Besides fear and material need, knowledge is one of the greatest incentives for followership. If you desire the respect and obedience of your employees, then you cannot stop educating yourself.

Chapter 6: Working Smart

The term "work smart" usually implies what you have been doing this whole time is essentially working "dumb." People often find this deduction in bad taste and are reluctant to even listen to the idea. In reality, nothing is demeaning about the notion of working smart. It is merely making improvements to a previous method of doing things. At a certain period in history, carriages were the most modern and comfortable forms of transportation. It spoke nothing negative about the intelligence of those who rode in them. When cars were invented society abandoned this now primitive way of travel for a much faster and luxurious vehicle. Now that people saw the possibilities, cars were just the smarter option.

Hopefully, this analogy puts you at ease with the idea of working smart. If you do a quick internet search you will find hundreds, if not thousands, of current websites detailing this process. While many of them are useful, you should ask yourself: does this help maximize my time? That question is the most important ideology behind working smart. For the foreseeable future, hard work will remain a factor for success. And the responsibilities of a manager are such that they can't afford to be lazy. Yet, even the most hardworking managers often find times where they are stressed and tired, and this fatigue rarely results in high productivity. If you identify this way, you should consider a different and more effective method.

A comprehensive study was done in 2018 to verify the claim that smart work leads to greater output. The work structure of about 5,000 professionals, including managers and other employees, was examined. The result proved that conventional hard (busy) work just doesn't cut it. The most effective workers were focused on value, as opposed to dividing their attention between every activity. They filter out the less crucial jobs for the day and target their energy towards the few important ones (Hansen, 2018). Again, this is the basis for working smart.

The major problem for those who decide to take this route is finding the courage to say no. Through years of societal conditioning, we've become convinced that getting involved in a lot of activities and always staying on the move is a great way to find fulfillment. But working smart encourages managers to delegate and collaborate more. The isolating pits that are typical of many work environments must be diminished, in favor of more alliances and cooperation.

Benefits of Smart Work

One of the most significant setbacks of busy work is how draining it is. Since today's world likes to romanticize and praise the fatigue caused by hard work, most managers remain silent or make jokes about the overwhelming levels of stress they endure. But this kind of stress and fatigue can lead to problematic health issues like heart disease and diabetes. They generally detract from the quality of life experienced by these overworked managers. While proactively maximizing your time does not imply that you can slack off, you would have more time in the day to relax and engage in non-work related activities.

Whichever approach you take to work, the end goal is the same for everyone: productivity. You want to be most effective and make a profit. This might seem like chasing the wind if you invest your energy in multitasking. The popular "hustle culture" that is touted by self-help gurus often charges us to do as much as possible for as long as we can manage before burning out. Supposedly, pushing our bodies, minds, and relationships to the very limit should lead to productivity. The sad truth is that very little is gained from overworking. Without taking a step back to evaluate your actions and target your energy towards more worthwhile jobs, you might find that you've made an insignificant amount of progress.

Managers who work smart are forced to be mentally present in all their activities. Since you're no longer trying to check every box, you can concentrate and notice a surge in your creativity. The more traditional hard work does not encourage innovation or deep thought. Instead, you are to routinely, and almost mindlessly, go about your tasks.

Your personal and professional life will be less haphazard by incorporating smart work tenets. It is the job of a manager to organize their employees and establish systems that lead to success. This might prove to be achievable if the manager cannot maintain a proper structure for their own lives. Indeed, one must adequately manage themselves before leading a team. Smart working managers organize their day and live by a forgiving yet effective system.

Smart Work Tips

Stop right where you are and think about this for a moment. If you are subscribed to the back-breaking, anxiety-inducing hustle mentality, the first thing you need to do now is stop. During this pause, try to meditate on what I just told you. You don't need to be on the floor or have your eyes closed to do this. If you can clear your mind and be attentive to just breathing, your current surroundings or the way your body is positioned is irrelevant. After a few (and maybe a few more) minutes of enjoying the blissfulness of doing nothing, proceed to evaluation.

Whether you choose to stop intentionally, you will be subjected to a variety of distractions during each day. You might be on social media longer than expected or engage in small talk. What is being encouraged here is a deliberate pause without relying on distractions to do so. Consider working offline more often. While receiving emails or Slack notifications might be an important form of communication for your company, you don't need to hear the ding each time something comes in. Social media notifications can also be a crippling distraction. Make sure to control or adjust these app notifications not only at work but in life. When you have time to quietly and peacefully collect your thoughts, review the day, and decide on the best way to spend your energy moving forward.

To effectively work smart, it's better to set short-term goals for yourself. If you think in the broad scope of, say, six years, you expose yourself to be engulfed by the myriad of unforeseen challenges and haste that seems to be the theme of this century. This also means that long-term goals make it difficult to stay positive. Instead, make personal and team goals for the day, some weeks, or a few months. This way, you are unlikely to be plagued by too many unknown factors, allowing you to stay focused on expected outcomes.

Timers are also a great way to forestall the pull of procrastination and laziness. You can try to race the clock. It not only makes you productive but is also a fun game. For example, make a list of small but important tasks that can be completed in 20 minutes or an hour. Do not beat yourself up if you do not make the time. Results of this little game are not indicative of any of your flaws. It's just a way to get you up and moving while deriving happiness from your job. If you must use things like software applications at work, make sure they aid your focus and boost productivity. There are some time management apps readily available on any iOS and Android devices. If you are able to find one that produces the right results, it is well worth the occasional glance at your phone or laptop. Also utilize post-it notes and other trivial office supplies. As basic as this product seems, it is a useful time management tool. When you move from one activity to the next at work, you may find yourself leaving behind a slew of unfinished jobs. While you plan to return to them eventually, there is always the possibility of either completely forgetting or just not remembering where you left off. By leaving notes, you can easily continue from where you left off and not have to spend time restrategizing. Try to plan the next day in advance. This is a great way to deal with stress and stay positive about your tasks. Spend the night (or day) before mapping out the next day. Psychologically, this gives you as much control as you can hope to have over your day.

While you do have some autonomy as a manager, it is advisable to check in with company heads on the jobs you are meant to prioritize. If your list is not congruent with the expectations of the higher-ups, all your efforts might not be received or appreciated the way you expect. As such, you cannot claim to have been working smart. Be concise in every action. Whether you're giving a speech to your employees, sending an email, or meeting with other leaders, you always want to whittle down your efforts to say and do only the most essential things. It's a no-brainer that when wasting other people's time, you are inadvertently wasting your own. By practicing brevity, it will soon become a part of your character, and this will help you make the most of your work day.

Reduce unimportant activities to routines. You may have likely seen or heard tech billionaire Mark Zuckerberg talk about the fact that he only buys and wears the same clothes each day to avoid the delay caused by decision-making. It is not necessary to go to this extreme. Brushing, bathing, preparing a meal, choosing an outfit, and certain office activities can be reduced to routines. If they are simple and repetitive tasks, you don't need to spend large portions of time on them.

Focus on the results and celebrate your accomplishments. This is opposed to pushing yourself to spend as much time as you can to get the most done. Reflect on what "little" you have done and celebrate *that* productivity. Think of all the times you waited until the last minute to meet a deadline. Somehow, you were able to do in a day what you couldn't achieve in a whole week. This phenomenon is called Parkinson's Law after the historian Cyril Northcote Parkinson, who provided this insight. It posits that the more time you are given to complete a relatively short task, the greater its complexity. Following the example above, this would mean that you only needed a day to complete the job. A week would just make it seem more daunting and cause you to be stressed.

With this knowledge, you do not have to request shorter deadlines. The ample legroom anticipates unforeseen issues that might cause you to need more time. You can give yourself less time to finish the job and make your plans around this self-imposed deadline. Please do not mistake this for procrastination. Most importantly, always make time to take care of your health. The entire purpose of maximizing your availability isn't just for job productivity. It should allow you the opportunity to look after yourself and enjoy what life brings.

You need adequate physical exercise, sleep, and proper nutrition. Should you become unwell, your productivity will very likely be negatively impacted. Spend more time on the activities you enjoy if you are able to do so. It is helpful as a stress management technique to start from doing things you love. Accomplishing them will make you feel appropriately challenged and fulfilled. Delegate other tasks to capable members of your team. This is one of the perks of being a manager, and it allows you to deal with the more critical business issues. It is also a display of trust in your employees. This confidence in their abilities acts as a boost in motivation and gets them to deliver their best. Delegation also tests the decision making and supervisory skills of managers. Such talents can only be honed with practice. So, do not hesitate to give more responsibilities to your workers. Of course, this should be done with consideration for their already existing workload. If, on the other hand, certain non desirable tasks cannot be delegated you must be disciplined enough to get them done. Disciplined managers don't fry their brains by stressing over tasks they don't like. That is why they can ultimately work for a long time and get things done. This is because they can find ways to keep their brains entertained and engaged. One of the ways to do this is by alternating through the steps. It goes like this: do the simple stuff for 15 minutes, do the hard stuff for 15 minutes, do the boring stuff for 15 minutes, and then do the exciting stuff for 15 minutes. This keeps your brain stimulated. You can change the time intervals into something you are more comfortable with, and you should take breaks in between. We will revisit this in the upcoming chapter.

Chapter 7: The Problem With Multitasking

When the topic of productivity and efficiency at work is discussed, you will hear multitasking is the best way to get everything done at once. Even with figures like Elon Musk supporting this style of operating, researchers continue to warn us about the dangers of trying to do numerous tasks at a time. There are many different degrees to multitasking. You might find it easy to make casual calls and scroll through social media all at once. However, the difficulty increases when you try to juggle various managerial activities. The goal in this scenario isn't merely to complete a task, albeit poorly executed. You want your best effort to shine through in the results.

As put forth by scientists, the human mind is not equipped to handle the load of heavy multitasking. The more activities you are engaged in, the more exposed you will be to distractions. In fact, studies show that multitaskers are 40% less productive than their more focused counterparts (Cherry, 2020). One reason for this is the time it costs to go from one task to the next. The study found that individuals who resumed the same duty could effectively continue much faster than those who were switching to a new one. The amount of lost time also increased significantly with the complexity of the job. This lost time may not be bothersome if you are performing house chores or passing time scrolling on the internet. But in the high stakes of a managerial position, it can quickly add to and lead to disastrous consequences.

Another problem with multitasking is how it hinders the ability to differentiate relevance from irrelevance. Every task is lumped together as the manager flits from one activity to the next in no particular order. As with any action, multitasking becomes a habit with repetition. This means that all the negative consequences of this behavior may occur, even when the individual attempts to focus on a single activity. In other words, the minds of multitaskers are often impaired to the point that they remain less effective than their focused peers in single tasks. (Nass, et al. 2009). This can be an especially scary fact for managers, from whom constant efficiency is required.

More Reasons to Stop Multitasking

1. It's akin to self-deceit to think that you can truly multitask. If you consider it literally, it is an impossible feat. Think of it as juggling. The number of objects you have in the air, your dexterity, and admirable powers of concentration do not matter in the definition of multitasking. At any point in time, you will always have one object in either hand. What you call multitasking is often just a frantic and harmful switch to various activities. Our brains, minds, and bodies are not engineered to cater to numerous tasks simultaneously. So, why waste useful time trying.

2. As a result of the fast-paced and preoccupied nature of multitasking, people who attempt it are usually left stressed and anxious. The more you try to fit into your plate, the less you can consume. This cycle can lead to several mental health issues. There is also the physicality that is involved in multitasking. Their lives appear to be in a constant state of "red alert." As is inevitable with such a degree of restlessness, multitaskers often experience raised

blood pressure. Should this set of individuals experience failure after this excessive effort, they might suffer damaging blows to their self-esteem or sink into depression.

3. Indeed, multitaskers are the most prone to errors. Getting your job done right demands concentration. And as a manager, you are not only watching out for your own mistakes but those of your employees. It would not be a problem if you misspelled a word on a status because you were listening to music and eating at the same time. However, you cannot afford the same mistakes when evaluating a report by your team member. Your mind must be present and focused, and multitasking is antithetical to concentration.

4. Eventually, all these issues pile up and weigh on your relationships. This could be your relationship with colleagues at work, friends, or family members. By placing enormous pressure on yourself to perform at work, you might neglect your loved ones. Also, multitasking managers often push this strategy on their employees. Since they are always busy (which may not translate to productivity), they expect to see their team members doing something—preferably, in a state of hurriedness.

5. Besides deteriorating mental health and poor relationships, multitasking can also lead to accidents. In fact, 25% of all vehicular accidents are caused by distracted drivers (Safestart, 2014). And many of these drivers are professionals trying to dial a call or check their email when they should be focused on the road. Accidents at work—even fatal kinds—can also be the result of distraction.

How to Properly Multitask

While it is not encouraged to multitask, there *are* a few benefits to this work style—as listed above. And this book would not be balanced if we discussed the negative aspects of multitasking alone. If you feel that it is within your ability to divide your attention between multiple activities and remain productive, then here are some ways to do it right.

1. Struggling with multitasking often starts when trying to juggle unrelated tasks. You need to convince your brain that the various tasks involved are the same type. By doing so, your memory is not impaired as your brain switches to different activities. Before you begin the day, you can write a multitask version of a to-do list, this will include all the crucial activities you have to get done at work. Categorize similar jobs together and refer to the list throughout the day.
2. To keep yourself constantly motivated, make sure that your to-do list is boldly visible. The distraction and stress of multitasking can be terribly damaging to your morale. As such, you should do whatever it takes—that is also healthy, of course—to maintain enthusiasm and confidence. Another benefit of the to-do list is it makes sure you do not forget anything in the chaos. So, put the list in the most attention-grabbing spot in your office. You may also want to write them in caps and use various colors.
3. The fact that you are multitasking is not an excuse to set unrealistic goals for yourself. You are still just a human being with about 9 to 11 work hours each day. Recognize your limits and give yourself the grace to not meet some of your daily targets. With time, you will learn to draw up a more feasible list of expectations.
4. You can also perform tasks in time blocks. It is also called the Pomodoro Technique. The rationale

behind this is that our minds function best in short stints. You might find it easier to focus and be productive for an hour than working two hours straight. As such, you need to figure out the optimum length of time for your concentration. You may then set a timer for 30 minutes and work without distractions. Once that time elapses, stop, and relax. This technique also encourages you to increase the length of your breaks after four blocks.

5. As a manager, you do not have to be actively involved in every task. As such, you have the opportunity to multitask uniquely. While some jobs may need you to be present, you can delegate others and only be involved as a supervisor. As relieving as this is, there are some obvious drawbacks. You may have to deal with the constant interruption of your team members. There are ways to work around this problem. You can delegate and use the Pomodoro Technique. With proper communication, your employees will understand your method and only reach out during your breaks. There are, of course, eventualities that one may not be able to schedule for. So, ensure that you are not too strict that your employees can't inform you of emergencies.

Chapter 8: Time Management

The discussion about multitasking rarely comes up when adequate planning is in place. Although managers recognize the need for to-do lists and other planning strategies, they often neglect time management. This much talked about skill is simply the ability of an individual to maximize their time. While an hour might seem insufficient to some, it can be effectively utilized by those who have spent the time building their time management skills. And this is accomplished without employing such unhealthy tactics as multitasking or a high intake of caffeine. For managers, this skill would extend to managing the time of their team members too.

One of the first things you would learn from time management is how much time to spend on specific tasks. We touched on a few aspects of this subject while discussing smart work and time blocks. Yet, this only touches the surface of everything time management entails. In this chapter, you will learn even more useful tips on how to productively organize your day. We will also outline the benefits of devoting your time to practicing time management skills.

Time Management Tips

Although one of the lesser-known techniques, the quadrant system can help to simplify planning. To do this, you write out four categories, into which you will list out your tasks for the day based on their importance (I) and urgency (U). For example, the first quadrant could list out activities that are both I and U. The second quadrant may contain activities that are neither I nor U. For the third quadrant, consider adding activities that are I but not U. You can add activities that are U but not I into the fourth quadrant. By following this step, it should be clear that you definitely want to stay away from the second quadrant. And, it would be wise to prioritize the first quadrant.

Evaluate the way you presently spend your time. Remember not to rush this process. You may even want to journal your findings. The questions you should answer might be some version of: "What do I spend the most time on?" or "How much do I get done each day?" After spending some time trying out the quadrant system, it is advisable to analyze how well it works for you. You may ask, "Which quadrant do I spend the most time on?"

You may have heard about the 80/20 rule. This technique, which is termed the Pareto Principle, claims that our most significant results often come from minimal effort. It provides that 20% of results come from 80% of effort and vice versa. Your responsibility is to figure out the 20% effort that yields the most results and scale it. Those are probably the jobs you either love or most trained to do. As a manager, you may then decide to delegate the others.

Intrinsic motivation is praised as the best way to inspire oneself. However, external rewards can be used to fuel internal motivation. Try to watch TED talks or similarly motivational/educational videos during those times you feel drained. Do what you can to ensure you don't lose the desire to meet your daily goals.

On a few occasions, you will find that not waiting to feel motivated is the more favorable option. You may, in fact, find the drive to complete an activity after you have started working. Regardless of feelings of uncertainty, do your part by getting up and let both momentum and adrenaline take care of the rest.

Decluttering your office space might seem unrelated to time management, but it is vital to staying focused and productive. When there is so much happening around you, it might be difficult to pay attention to the things that matter. As you know by now, your ability to concentrate is directly proportional to productivity. So, properly arrange the disorganized papers and other stationery. In fact, the more clean and empty spaces in your office, the better for your focus.

Benefits of Time Management

You will have more time to bond with your employees. Getting to know your team members on a personal level can only happen if everyone is calm and relaxed. If there is never enough time to ask your teammates about how they are feeling and listen to their suggestions, the work environment might feel like an autocracy. If you and your employees have ample time to complete tasks, there will be fewer mistakes or the need for time-consuming revisions. Since these errors can snowball into missed deadlines and extra work, you would be leading a truly productive team by managing time.

In every company, there is always that employee whose competence is questioned. Even though this individual is qualified for the job, their results are inconsistent. And as such, leaders find it hard to trust them with responsibilities. For managers, their team members may be unsure about following their lead. This inconsistency is often the result of poor time management. By successfully maximizing your day, you will gain a reputation that will result in lucrative opportunities. There will be no doubt in the minds of your superiors that you will promptly deliver every time. In addition, your employees will admire your work ethic and respect your leadership.

It has become kind of a cliché for interviewers to ask where one sees themselves in X amount of years. The common response is a plain statement or the interviewee confessing they have no idea what the future holds for them. While it is true that no human being or machine can accurately predict the future, time management can afford us some insight into how things may turn out. Even with the curve balls that life likes to throw you, an individual with good time management skills can still plan out their future and realize goals in record time.

Procrastination is one of the most alluring yet deceptive phenomena in life. This is especially true for professionals. The desire to "do it later" is one of the hallmarks of a procrastinator. Practicing time management skills enforces the habit of diligence. And this effectively eliminates the self-limiting behavior that is procrastination.

Time management also creates a harmonious team. The relationship that exists between your team members is just as important—maybe, even more important—as the manager (you), have with them. It is not enough that they respect and consider you to be relatable. They must also respect and be kind towards each other. This might be hard to achieve in a haphazard and chaotic environment. Without time management, arguments might become a constant feature among your team members.

Chapter 9: Manipulation

It is unarguable that workplace manipulation creates a toxic work environment for you. Apart from impacting your productivity, it also has implications on mental and emotional health. It is often typical for people working in such environments to come home drained and joyless. Furthermore, these categories of persons are the ones likely to dread each coming week. The built-up anxiety over time might even result in a break-down, and in that way affecting other relationships that the person has.

Considering how harmful the effects of workplace manipulation is, it is hence surprising that sometimes people won't recognize signs of workplace manipulation. This could be due to one of two reasons. The first is that workplace manipulation, or manipulation tactics in general, are not immediately conspicuous. They are most times overt, and thus while you may realize that a certain co-worker, or that your boss makes you uncomfortable, you may not know exactly the reasons for that. The other reason is acceptance. Manipulation tactics tend to be incremental, growing over time. A person who works in such an environment keeps making room to accommodate them that eventually, they get used to it. Thus, these manipulative tactics seep into the work-culture of that particular workplace, and such a person may find themselves unable to identify or get up from under its effects.

Identifying the signs of workplace manipulation is crucial because it aids a person to overcome it. If you suspect that you work in an environment where manipulation is the norm rather than the exception, you may want to look out for these signs to be sure of the next steps.

Signs of Workplace Manipulation

1. **Dreading Monday**. Granted, most people suffer from some version of the Monday blues when working a nine to five. This is due, in no small part, to the fact that most individuals only make use of the weekend for decompressing and relaxation. And this requires more than a full 48 hours. So, when the weekend is over, they find themselves inadequately prepared for the challenges of the new week. Having the Monday blues every once in a while is not bad and is actually expected. The more stressful or demanding your job is, the more intensely you will feel the Monday blues when they come.

   It becomes deeply problematic when you feel anxiety about your work more often than not. You should be concerned if you find that you often dread going to work or stress working with a particular person. You may not know the exact cause of these responses. However, if the concerns are serious enough to warrant such an emotional rollercoaster, you need to pay attention and try to find the root.

2. **You feel devalued**. Any environment where you feel undervalued or unappreciated can become toxic fast. In the workspace, your opinions and contributions should count for something. The idea is that you are helping your team achieve a common goal by contributing your own quota. Hence, when you are told, subtly or even openly, that you are not pulling your own weight, or that the contributions you are making do not matter, which is certainly a cause for alarm.

For instance, if you are used to hearing statements like "Wow that's stupid," "You always bring up weird ideas," or "Why did you ever think that would work?" you most likely are thick in the middle of a manipulative environment. Also, your bosses or colleagues may try to belittle your achievements. They could make it appear as though you did not really work for any achievement you recorded or it was just luck that worked out in your favor.

Additionally, you may see the signs in the nonverbal cues they portray. They may have the habit of not looking at you or looking past you when you are speaking or while they are talking to you. You might also notice that when you are making contributions in a team meeting, for example, they take that opportunity to start looking at their phones or to start up a conversation with someone else present and distract others as well. All of these are signs of being undervalued and can affect your psyche and sense of self-worth.

3.   **Silent treatment**. This is a sign of a manipulative workplace environment and is mostly employed by bosses. Here, you might find a leader constantly ignoring you. Your calls, texts, and emails go unanswered without explanation for cause for such rude behavior. You might even find that you are being singled out for this treatment and every other person in the office receives a prompt response to texts and emails. The idea here is to keep you flustered and bewildered. This is particularly true if you report to said leader, and require his feedback in certain situations. Manipulative bosses employ this skill as a type of power trip. With it, they intend to display how indispensable they are and keep you always leaning on them for support. Whenever you notice that this is the case with you and a superior, you need to tread carefully. You might just be working in a toxic and manipulative workplace.

4.   **Fact distortion**. Any workplace where colleagues cannot hold each other to the basic standards of honesty is

definitely manipulative. Manipulative people are quite adept at avoiding questions, making excuses, and embellishing the truth. They are quick to tell lies, withhold vital information, or just give you half-truths. Sometimes they tell these lies to cover their tracks and prevent their unscrupulous activities from coming to light. This is because manipulative bosses are often slothful and given to not putting in their best at work.

5.   **Lack of empathy**. Granted, your boss and co-workers do not have to be your best friends as these work relationships are expected to be formal. However, someone does not have to be your family to deserve empathy and understanding. More importantly, you can also be productive in an environment where you feel seen, have your struggles and limitations appreciated, and get praise for work well done. In a manipulative workplace environment, co-workers and bosses deliberately weaponize their lack of empathy as a trick to get to others. If your boss does not let you take time off, your colleagues refuse to help you out on tasks when they can, etc. You may be working in an environment where there is a lack of empathy.

> Another area you may witness a lack of empathy could be in the demands made by your boss. When they place unreasonable demands on you, they expect you to fail, giving them a reason to berate you further. Thus, you have to take a careful look at the tasks you are being assigned. Can you match the expectations of those demands? Can you effectively carry out the task without feeling drained afterward? Are these demands consistent? Your answers to these questions will indicate whether you are working in a manipulative environment or not.

Manipulation Techniques

Many types of manipulative people exist in the workplace, in your family, and in each social setting. The tactics they employ will also vary. In any case, exhaustive deliberation on them all might be impossible. However, a careful look at some of the most popular ones will give you a fair idea of what to expect and how to tackle them when they arise.

1. **Smear campaigns**: This is a deliberate control of your narrative by a third party. It borders on slander, and the intention is to punch holes in your reputation. The technique here is simple for a toxic person, if they cannot break you, they'll get others to see you as broken. Thus, this sort of person would go through great lengths to control how others see you. They will project all your 'not-so-great' traits before others, pitching you as incompetent, foolish, or wicked.

   In some instances, a toxic person might go as far as pitting two groups against each other. Thus, you have to be watchful when a colleague or friend constantly comes to you with tales of another's failure or inadequacies. It can also be that this person likes to regale you with tales of what someone said about you, regardless of it being praise or criticism. You have to be careful. This person may be (and is likely) doing the same thing to the other person. They may not have your best intentions at heart or are hoping to trick you into giving them information or to spark a fight.

2. **Gaslighting**: This is perhaps one of the most common manipulation techniques there is. Here, the manipulator wants you to question your reality. They distort facts, and after the argument or altercation, you end

up worrying whether you are crazy. At the end of it, victims no longer trust their memories or perceptions.

3.   **Projection**: This is a little like gaslighting in that the manipulator intends to have the person question their own version of events. Here, they transfer their negative traits to the other person. The victim labors under the mistaken assumption that they caused whatever problems are existing around them. Narcissists and psychopaths commonly employ this tactic. They hardly ever take responsibility for any of their actions and would rather shift the blame on to a third party. They are extremely methodical and logical; thus, when they are done providing an alternative explanation for the cause of the problem, you might even end up believing it yourself

4.   **Cruel sarcasm**: Manipulation techniques that are the most effective are those that are subtle, such as sarcasm. Toxic people look for the times your guards are down to launch an attack. They make jokes without the intention of making you smile. These jokes are either to create a chink in your armor or to put you down before others.

> Of course, you must understand that some people make cruel jokes without intending any harm. Some find it difficult to draw the line between what is socially acceptable and what is frowned upon. Thus, they are bound to hurt the feelings of those around them without knowing or meaning to. While the worst accusation you could pin on these people is cluelessness, toxic individuals take this to a whole new level. If you are unsure about a person's intentions, observe their actions in each scenario. If a person exhibits a pattern of cruel jokes primarily intended to put you down or make you feel bad while projecting themselves, they most likely are being manipulative.

5.   **Baiting**: Manipulators are masters of baiting. They deliberately put up acts to rile you up. Their actions might include taking jabs at you or making cruel comments about

subjects you consider sensitive. When you rise to take the bait and react as any other person would in this circumstance, they would then point to your reaction as evidence that you are being irrational.

In the vast majority of these cases, they end up playing the victim. Without a thorough insight into the situation, onlookers would be quick to blame you. In fact, in recounting the incident, the manipulator would usually claim that your response was disproportionate to the provocation. It will then lead you to question your grip on your emotions and whether you are overreacting to situations. This further impacts your rationality and your overall mental health.

6.   **Moving the goalpost**: This manipulative tactic is best understood if you have a little knowledge about football. A goalpost is a mark that a person is supposed to reach. In an argument or discourse, a goalpost is a burden needed to be offset by either side using evidence or logic. However, when dealing with a toxic person, as soon as one goalpost is reached, the manipulator shifts gears, introducing new elements to the mix, making it difficult to hold them accountable. Thus, for a toxic person, nothing you do or say will be sufficient. If you engage with them on this level, you will be perpetually running circles around them, looking to meet their demands or ceaseless expectations. Of course, you will eventually fail, which is the intention of the manipulator. They will be quick to latch on to this failure as evidence of any conceived failings they have conjured up.

Be smart and recognize these tricks for what they are. Refusing to engage with the tricks and games employed by these persons is one way to deny them the power they claim to wield over you.

Persuasion and Not Manipulation

The first distinction between these concepts lies in their intention. Manipulation is often selfish. The purpose of using manipulative tactics is rarely ever to the benefit of the victim. Persuasion, some would argue, is neutral in this aspect. It does not work for specific benefits of either party. In this way, it can be seen as a more honorable way to convince another person to do things. This neutrality is strongly debated. However, we can all agree that coercion is rarely ever a factor in persuasion. Instead, the individual who is being persuaded fully understands that they have other choices besides the one presented to them. Of course, it will not be persuasion if you do not try to influence that choice. The only difference is that you are not employing such dark means as gaslighting and mockery to get your way. Instead, you offer stronger arguments.

We are persuaded to take specific action all the time. This method is used in internet ads and by politicians to influence our behavior. Managers can also be persuasive in the way they communicate with their employees. You need to understand these two rules as someone's boss.

1. Only focus your energy on persuading those who are already inclined to accept your point of view. Even though no one has immunity from persuasion, you would be more likely to quickly convince someone who is persuadable in the light of your idea. If you don't mind spending a much longer time trying to persuade people, then you can disregard this principle.

2.   Your timing can be damaging or beneficial to your ability to influence. You cannot hope to convince anyone of anything when they are busy. This is even more true when the activity in question is completely unrelated to what you are talking about. You will be more successful when the person you are attempting to persuade is not distracted.

3.   Appeal to the needs of your employees. This also includes doing them favors or reciprocating a kind deed. If you're known as the dependable and kind boss, your team members would be more likely to yield to your powers of persuasion. When you perform a favor, your employees will feel obligated to return it. And when you reciprocate one, you will appear more trustworthy.

Chapter 10: Terminating Team Members

A dancer's training is not complete if they have not figured out how to end it with grace and finesse. This means that the manner in which you let go of an employee matters just as much as the relationship you had cultivated with them in the past. The fact that you are letting them go does not have to mean you burn this bridge. There are numerous reasons besides incompetence or a lack of adequate qualifications for termination. Often, employees just don't fit the culture of your company, or financial strain necessitates letting go of some individuals. If you are not a hiring manager, you may not be involved in the process of employing new workers. This would mean that you are presented with these different personalities and must decide if you can work with them or not.

The termination process is important in its own right as it sends a message to the rest of the team. They can glean, from the way you handle such issues, how the company values them. Also, the individual who will be leaving the company is a human being whose mental and emotional health should be treated with care. In addition, you can never be certain that they won't be of some crucial help to you in the future.

Use the steps below as a guide when you decide to terminate an employee.

1. Be immediately upfront and clear about your intentions. These situations are typically awkward, and as a result, you might feel compelled to beat around the bush, put it off, and use unclear terms. You might consider this to be a gentle tactic, but it does no one any favors. In fact, the employee might get confused and feel even more devastated when they finally understand that they are losing their job. You can place yourself in their shoes (that is, empathize with their situation). Would you appreciate the needless suspense or prefer a more direct approach?
2. Although there is no way to soften the blow, you want to make sure that the dignity of the employee remains intact. Do not be careless in the way you break this news to them. More importantly, it should not be done to the hearing of the other workers. This saves the employee in question from humiliation, and prevents an atmosphere of fear in the workplace. You cannot expect your workers to feel secure in their position after seeing a colleague, one they probably really cared about, get fired.

3. As a result of the legal consequences of behaving unethically while terminating an employee and wrongful termination, you are advised to have a witness present. This witness should, preferably, be an HR representative. They could also be a lawyer or an employee who has a credible reputation in the company. Such situations can get so tense that the employee might attempt to hurt you. This is why some managers opt for a police escort as a witness. In this way, you would be protecting yourself from lawsuits as well as bodily harm.

4. Whether you have your lawyer as a witness while firing workers, it is imperative that you consult their expertise before making this decision. There are numerous ways to wrongfully fire an employee, and you are probably ignorant about a few of them. One of the things your lawyer would do is meticulously read the employment contract that the worker has with your company. They should advise you against firing the worker for reasons that are not stated in the contract; one of such reasons might be a medical leave.

5. Always give prior warning. There really is no way to adequately prepare someone for losing their jobs, but you can make sure that you do not voice your dissatisfaction with their effort at the same time as you let them go. Give them the opportunity to improve. It is advised that companies do a performance review every year. It would not be in excess to review the performance of your employees more than twice a year. Oftentimes, the need to fire an employee is eliminated by a performance review. This is because the worker knows which areas they are underperforming and how they can do better. If there is still no obvious improvement, you can resort to firing. The employee would be less surprised by your action and you can present the reviews to back up your decision.

Of course, you do not have to go through this process if the worker has violated company policy.

For instance, it is perfectly understandable to immediately fire an employee who has been proven to sexually harass someone in the office.

6.   It should be done in person. There is no argument that this is one of the most awkward conversations you will ever have. But if you cannot delegate the responsibility to someone else, then refrain from firing your employee over the phone or through social media. Even a well-crafted email will not suffice. Although you are delivering hurtful news, you want to communicate that you care about them on a personal level, and that this only has to do with business and numbers. Those second-hand channels do carry the same courtesy or intimacy as a face to face conversation. This is even more important if the employee has been working with the company for a long time. Hostility is more likely to surface when you treat such a situation with carelessness and disrespect.

7.   Regardless of the emotions displayed by your worker, you must keep yours in check. They might cry or become violent, but you must be mindful of your reaction. You don't want to be distant or seem unsympathetic. In fact, this is one of the best times to show empathy. However, you should be careful about coming close to the employee or touching them. While your only intentions might be to offer comfort and deescalate a tense situation, this could lead to harassment suits or bodily injuries. If the embittered employee resorts to insults, do not return the harsh words. Simply wish them well and maintain a calm composure.

8.   It works best if the conversation is kept to a minimum. Rehashing your previously mentioned displeasure with their job will only increase the likelihood of anger, abusive words, and violent behavior. It is only expected that the employee will want to know why their job is being terminated. And you *should* answer their questions. This is another reason why performance reviews are so important. It allows you to speak succinctly in such situations. You can answer like this: your performance, as pointed out in the several reviews, does not fit our standards. You needn't explain further. Just wish them success in their future employment.

9.   A common mistake made by some managers during terminations is to create the impression that the decision isn't final. They hope that by using vague terms, the employee will take the news calmly. The individual might remain calm, but it could be for entirely different reasons. You might, inadvertently, send the message that they have the chance to change your mind. This is misleading, and actually a much crueler approach. While it may not appear like it, the kind approach is to be courteous and direct. Once you have exchanged pleasantries with the employee, plainly tell them the purpose of the meeting.

10.   You should maintain control over the employees' access to their workspace. They, in fact, should not be allowed to meet the other employees. This is even more necessary if the worker is visibly shaken and angry about the termination. Vengeful employees might leave with sensitive company documents or cause a disturbance among their former team members. Offer to have their personal items sent to their homes. Should they refuse, you can let them clear out their office during the lunch break or over the weekend. Another reason for restricting the employee's contact with other workers is to help save face. Make it a priority to protect the dignity of the individual who has lost their job.

11.   This restriction must also be done electronically. They should not be allowed to access things like the company email and customer forums. There are real instances of employees causing damage to a company's system or reputation after losing their employment. Before firing the employee, you will need to inform the IT department of your company. Stripping the employee of access and informing them about their job termination should be done at the same time.

12.   If the employee's conduct was not outrageous, it is encouraged to give them a financial boost to help with their future endeavors. The meeting does not have to end on a sad or disagreeable note. Firing an employee should serve the interests of all parties involved. While your company saves resources that would have been wasted on a bad fit, the employee can move on to more productive and fulfilling ventures. If they seem to take the termination well, briefly

discuss future job opportunities with them. Your word as their past employer might be useful in helping them get a new job. In essence, you should encourage them to believe that they will find a more fitting employment or career path. Remember: all these should be said and done with brevity.

13.   To aid the smoothness of this process, it might be necessary to have a checklist. The points listed above in this chapter and any others you can come up with should be in the checklist. You should be careful that the discussion does not end up being mechanical or clinical. Use the checklist as a guide to avoid forgetting important topics during the termination.

When to Terminate an Employee

The points below do not cover all the possible reasons for relieving an employee of their job. However, take them into consideration before making such a final decision. Should any of your team members exhibit these behaviors, it might be best to let them go.

They apologize but do not change. After sharing the results of a performance review with your workers, what you want more than apologies is a correction of the poor behavior. Give them enough time to make the necessary changes. If any team member remains obstinate, then you needn't bother with extra chances.

You've been thinking about terminating them. This is not the same as going with your gut feeling. There are individuals whose persistent actions warrant the termination of their employment, and you have spent a while pondering how to let them go without blowback. Your performance as a manager can be negatively affected if you are forced to deal with an employee who you would rather see gone. Seek the advice of the HR department and release the worker.

They affect team spirit. As much as you want to be a good person, you cannot afford an employee whose personality or behavior dampens the morale of the other workers. Even if that worker is especially competent, they should not be allowed to undermine the rest of the staff. You should take note of team morale and see if it increases when certain individuals are not around.

They blatantly violate company policies. There are often those employees who are brazen in their defiance of established rules and regulations. This is usually not a result of ignorance. If they break obvious policies concerning weapons at work or sexual harassment, then three-strike chances and performance reviews can be overlooked. Your company would fare a lot better without such characters, and their jobs should be immediately terminated. Before terminating an employee based on these reasons, remember to find evidence that they really did violate policy.

Their actions affect productivity. Every member of your team needs to get their job done for jobs to progress smoothly. For example, if one member is a chronic procrastinator, this aspect of their character might negatively impact the productivity of the entire team. Again, you do not want this behavior to damage the morale of your workers.

They enjoy discord. As already pointed out in this book, one of the responsibilities of a manager is to encourage unity among the members of your team. You are expected to make decisions that would help your workers play well. Unfortunately, you might have an employee who seems to thrive on disunity and drama. It often seems like they disrespect and hurt the feelings of their colleagues on a whim. While there are skills in the armory of experienced managers to help in dealing with various personalities, you are not a psychotherapist. As such, the best solution for this problem might be to release the employee.

They just don't care. When it has to do with productivity, the worst kind of employees are the apathetic kind. They seem disinterested in their job and their coworkers, and do not put in the needed effort. You may try to figure out the reason for their lackluster performance. However, you should not hesitate to terminate them if this behavior persists.

Conclusion

At this point, it is safe to assume that you are a manager who cares about the numbers indicating good performance, and the wellbeing of your employees. You want them to be effective *and* happy at work. This is why you have taken the time to read this book and reflect on your own habits.

The next step would be to apply all you have learned to the betterment of your team. Hopefully, you have already started practicing the introspection and self-awareness that will help you be a more confident and empathetic leader. Be more attentive towards some of the personal issues of your team members and approach every challenge with calmness and kindness. Also, decide on a management style and stay consistent. In no time, your employees will recognize your strength, stability, and effectiveness as a leader. They will respect you more for it, striving to emulate the same courtesy and kindness that you display adding it to their own repertoire for everyday life.

References

Cherry, L. (2020, March 26). *How multitasking affects productivity and brain health.* Verywell Mind. **https://www.verywellmind.com/multitasking-2795003**

Hansen, M. (2018, June 20). *Working smart—defined by a study of over 5000 managers and employees.* Thrive Global. **https://thriveglobal.com/stories/working-smart-defined-by-a-study-of-over-5-000-managers-and-employees**

Le Phan, L. (2018, November 8). *15 unmistakable qualities of bad managers.* Kununu Blog. **https://transparency.kununu.com/unmistakable-qualities-of-bad-managers/**

Nass, C., Ophir, E., & Wagner, A. D. (2009). Cognitive control in media multitaskers. *PNAS USA, 106(37), 15583-15587.* **https://doi.org/10.1073/pnas.0903620106**

Nazar, J. (2012). *The 21 principles of persuasion.* Forbes. **https://www.google.com/amp/s/www.forbes.com/sites/jasonnazar/2013/03/26/the-21-principles-of-persuasion/amp/**

Rochas, P. (2003). Five levels of self-awareness as they appear early in life. *Consciousness and Cognition, 12(4),* 31-717. **https://doi:10.1016/S1053-8100(03)00081-3**

Spratt, E. G., Friedenberg, S. L., Swenson, C. C., et al. (2012). The effect of early neglect on cognitive, language, and behavioral functioning in childhood. *Psychology, 3(2),* 175-182. **https://doi:10.4236/psych.2012.32026**

Stevenson, R. (2018, February 17). *5 ideal reasons why random acts of kindness are so important.* Ideal.

https://idealmagazine.co.uk/5-reasons-random-acts-kindness-important/

Top 10 causes of distracted driving—and what they all have in common. (2014, July 10). Safestart. **https://safestart.com/news/top-10-causes-distracted-driving-and-what-they-all-have-common/#:~:text=It's%20no%20surprise%20that%20distracted,a%20result%20of%20distracted%2 odriving**.